AF448559

the
longest
way
around,
the
quickest
way
home.

"I wish you a kinder sea."

-*Emily Dickinson*

table of contents

growing pains

the more i take my life into my own hands,
the more they tremble.
i'm so scared to be alone,
scared to be alive
sometimes.

i've been wrong about so much of all this -
i thought my body was my friend and it isn't,
i thought you would stay and you didn't.

i gambled on the safest bets and i still lost the game;
i used to be so confident and now there is only shame,
held my cards close to my chest but was cheated all the same.

time is supposed to heal all wounds but it only drives me
farther away from when i felt alright,
who'd have thought that the things i thought were victories
were actually warning signs?
you make yourself a target when the world no longer expects
you to put up a fight.

i understand that change is often born of necessity
and not desire,
i try to keep up with the innovation but i am so very tired,
it feels like it's been ages since i've been truly inspired.

what doesn't kill you only ignites resentment,
i no longer want to be resilient;
i am not the person i used to be, but there are remnants.

the closer i get to clarity the more it seems even farther,
and my posture suffers from years of trying to make myself
smaller;
a sense of childhood whimsy uselessly preserved; never
explored, never bothered.

i have to reach a place that can no longer contain me before
i am able to expand,
but these growing pains make shaky legs unable to stand;
i'm a stranger within my own body in the reflection of the
glass.

change is mandatory
but is the pain?
has all of it been in vain?
tell me it'll all be okay -

i never wanted to grow up this way.

one little victory

i would tell you that i love you but i'm not sure
i know what that means
this is me trying to explain it somewhat articulately -

just be patient with me, please
i'm still learning how to be somebody that someone might be
afraid to leave.

and how do i get rid of the sting?
why i can't i remember the last time i felt clean?

lately it's like no one can see how badly i'm breaking,
like they can't see these fickle hands shaking.

sweeping up shards of a sweet broken dream
we both know you aren't coming home but i'll still save you
a glittering, grimy piece.

don't cry for me, i'll bite my tongue even as it gets harder
and harder to breathe,
because i've been trained to people-please.

every time i try to fight i end up on my knees
i honestly think i'd be okay if i could just have

one
little
victory

atonement

you learn to tread lightly
in a house full of keepsakes
heirloom china falls, shatters, breaks
a shoebox full of memories you cannot bring yourself to
face

sheets cover up the furniture
linen gathers dust
old picture frames begin to fade and rust
nothing holds more weight than all of this history does

the floorboards creak in cluttered chorus
dishes sit unwashed
a magnet-clad fridge has been abandoned fully stocked
damning evidence of a dream too hastily lost

wilting plants and humid air turned stale
cryptographs for someone else to find
the patterned bedsheets under which you used to hide
in retrospect, the wallpaper looks more yellow than it
ever did white

nostalgia leaves and in its place melancholy lingers
and time passes nonetheless
taking with it all the things you wish you'd said;
all of the opportunities that came and left
achingly hollow walls sentenced to a lifetime of
lonely guests

the blue is eternal

the sunrise looms with graying dew
a hazy sepia tints the memories of you

green with envy and grass that glides along skin
i ache to feel the yellow light surround me once again

it has been noticeably absent since your departure
yet remains no match for the blackening resentment i harbor

the humble beginnings of a spark gather into an artificial flame
we cannot bask forever in the golden light of day

a dark indigo thunderstorm rolls in overhead
while my mind replays a vignette of all the words you said

it is my mistake for hoping to see you after the evening
rain clears
a blank white canvas of clouds mirrors my desolate fears

i'm left to admire the red of the sunset's burn
where the iron-rust orange meets the browning dirt below

and i wade for a while in the never ending purple
but this blue -

this blue is the only thing that seems eternal.

two wrongs don't make

a right

we were both wrong if i'm being honest
nobody gets anywhere thinking in black & whites
i never managed to leave the place we grew up in
and you've had your suitcases packed since you were five.

i made it clear that i couldn't go with you
and you swore that you had to leave
it still stings to think about when you admitted
the world might have more to offer you than me.

so maybe i should be more open to exploring
but maybe you shouldn't be so quick to set things aside
either way, we should've known from the beginning
that two wrongs don't make a right.

scar tissue

when you're hurt in the same spot over and over scar tissue
begins to build up
like it's trying to protect the bones beneath
like a rubber band coiled up underneath the skin
more stubborn than i expected it to be

pulled taut and sore like an overextended tendon
you'd think the extra layer would give me some thicker skin
invisible to the untrained eye
but all it does is radiate pain, become more sensitive

once it's no longer visible it's difficult to tell
without reopening the wound
and you begin to wonder if it even actually happened -
if your mind has manipulated the truth

the bruise becomes lighter
the cut heals
the evidence fades
but the scar tissue
never goes away

when it rains, it pours

i've never been one for cautionary metaphors
they say when it rains it always pours
this thunderstorm is what i get for loving
a drowning heart like yours

by now

i thought i'd be decorating an apartment somewhere
in the city,
with polaroids i took on late nights with my friends.
i thought i'd be buying my own groceries,
crafting new beginnings & mourning nostalgic ends.

to be honest i thought we'd stay together;
balancing expectation with reality is a skill i've yet to master.
i have a hard time leaving well enough alone,
and i go insane trying to identify the patterns.

i knew that life was going to be difficult,
but i thought things would be easier than this.
one minute i'm fine and the next i'm falling apart,
and sometimes i can't tell what the difference is.

to be young is to have the world at your fingertips but
also on your shoulders,
to wish you were younger the more you get older,
and if i could've warned my former self i would've told her
the world's a frigid place, just do your best not to make it an
colder.

the lights are still on in the house that i grew up in
but the people we used to be are long gone,
buried somewhere in the backyard under the tall trees
while our weary ghosts stumble on.

i thought that by now i'd be healing
and moving on with my life,
but all i've encountered thus far
are weathered paperbacks of goodbyes.

suture

people marvel at the existence of a heart beating
outside of a body
but i'm the one that's doomed to pay the price
losing pieces of it every time its handed off
with no consolation prize

to put it simply;
i have things and then i don't
and i spend years trying to suture the leftover holes

just because

just because something is true doesn't mean it's the only solution / just because it's a valid point doesn't mean it won't be disputed / just because things are bad doesn't mean they'll be that way forever / just because the sun isn't shining doesn't mean there will always be poor weather.

just because i'm smiling doesn't mean i'm truly happy / just because you want me doesn't mean you already have me / just because you say the words doesn't mean that you're in love / i learned the hard way that the real thing never quite measures up.

just because i tried it doesn't mean that i'll succeed / just because i struggle doesn't mean that i need you to intervene / just because i planned it one way doesn't mean it'll all work out / these days if there's no one around to see the victory, does it really even count?

just because i'm different than you doesn't mean
that i'm no good / just because i thought i said it clearly
doesn't mean i was understood / just because i want
something doesn't mean it's a guarantee / but wouldn't it
be nice just once not to survive solely on my needs?

just because i know all of this doesn't make the pill
easier to swallow / just because nothing's going to change
doesn't mean i'm looking forward to what follows / just
because i feel indebted to everyone doesn't mean i have to
stick to the script / but even in saying this right now i
already know that i will.

sandcastles

the sunset is invitingly deceiving
and the humid air feels stale
you drive us there in calculated silence
with not a shred of reassurance to spare

you threw me in the deep end
i call out but you won't take my hand
i'm choking on the salt water
while you build castles in the sand

i've ruined your vacation
with the ballasts chained to my legs
i am a shipwreck waiting to be explored
left undiscovered in the end

i'm sorry to have to tell you this
but i fear i'm drowning once again
the darkness is beginning to tempt me
and the currents carve craters into my pruned skin

exhaustion runs deep to my marrow
i don't feel like myself anymore
i barely manage to drag my soaking limbs
from the depths of the sea to the burning shore

i hear echoes in a seashell
of you counting up the days
you wish that i would break the rules
but good girls never change

is your castle built for both of us
or is it just me locked inside?
i watch as you get angry
as it's crushed beneath my tide

this time when the waves overtake me
please don't feel obligated to mourn;
i promise not to hold my breath
i am your burden no more

you load up the car to drive home
with an empty passenger seat
the sun rises and we are both so much lighter
now that we're finally free

resilient heart

the sad and unpleasant truth
of all of today's youth
is that most never even
saw themselves living
to seventeen or twenty-one or twenty-five
at least not in this lifetime.

but if no one else has told you
i am proud of you for making it this far
i know that it hasn't been easy
with your lovely, resilient heart.

jack-o-lantern

carve me like a jack-o-lantern
empty out my insides
go through all of the carnage
and tell me of the horrors you find

i exist more so in theory
than anything that's real
a fixture you bring out for holidays
then back to the attic for another year

light a candle for me
to illuminate what you've done
put me on display
my smile is a jagged, crooked one

you scraped out pieces of me
discarded like waste on your floor
with hands so cruel and careless
i am at your mercy; hollow forevermore

fault lines

my fault lines are internal
running throughout my veins
a parade of endless grievances
that cease at the sound of your name

i begged you to settle down with me
though my landscape was serrated
i asked you to turn a blind eye
to the chaos we created

i crumbled at the first sign of conflict
as if searching for a reason to erupt
my jagged edges pierced and scraped;
i hadn't known all i was capable of

i suppose i cannot blame you
for choosing to run while you still could
lest my desire to have you all to myself
have slaughtered you where you stood

yet still i find it difficult to admit to you, even now
that i would have loved you unevenly;
because i was a fault line with years of pressure
built up beneath the surface
and i was angry you did not want to build your home in me

some people

some people would do whatever it takes
and some people just take what they want

some people spend their time waiting for a heart to open
that never really does

some people are full of love
and some people just love themselves

some people are breaking down
without ever asking for help

some people yearn for company
and some people ache to be alone

some people spend their entire lives
searching for something that feels like home

yesterday's smile

you say *in five years, where do you want to be?*
but my brain doesn't work that way
i can't even calculate the trajectory of the next five minutes
will i be right here next to you or a million miles away?

hollow laughter and a counterfeit grin
i wonder if you can see through the act
it's meticulously scripted and rehearsed
on the list of my own priorities, why am i always last?

i put in the effort in the moment
but all of this optimism never pays off
all i am now is exhausted and lonely
how do i teach myself to slow down, to breathe, to stop?

my happiness is only borrowed
from a memory that resides out of my reach
yesterday's smile is nothing but today's sorrow
how do i explain that i feel like i'm not who i'm supposed
to be?

you say *in five years, where do you want to be?*
i really only have one answer:
not where i am now.
after hundreds of grim befores, i'm aching for a
happily ever after.

frost

they say it's about the journey but to change i am opposed
too afraid the space i carve out might be the wrong one
too nervous to choose a path at the fork in the road
too paralyzed to forge my own
worried that all of my progress may be unraveled, undone.

each time i think i've arrived at the very end
there is something else i've got to choose
there is another direction i would not have thought to descend
there is another obstacle around the bend
but what have i got left to lose?

so i wait for a while at the spot where they diverge
as i weigh out the profundity of my options
as my thoughts and the trees disperse
as i attempt to extract some sort of a lesson learned
i pray my decision won't be too costly.

even though i struggle to pick sides i know i cannot have both
i won't let myself drag behind
i gather up my heart & my hope
i willingly choose the longer way home
determined to make it mine.

silver linings

this crimson running through me has proved itself contrite
coursing through labyrinth veins;
i am petrified to find that all i have left
is a compendium of numbered days.

it slips by unbidden, brown and neutral time
though the clock has long since frozen;
i've never liked the taste of coffee,
but i need something to keep me from the haze.

this is a deep blue everest i never chose to climb
and unfortunately i must do so alone;
my instructions arrived frail & useless,
desultory and terribly vague.

i struggled to accept the fate to which i'd been assigned
and felt it deeply unfair;
a haze of glowing amber in the distance
illuminating the silhouette of reckless mistakes.

i tumbled into suffocating deep sage vines
and became tangled in the hallows;
i ignored each of the signs
for which i had ardently prayed.

you can't survive in black and whites
but oh;
it is so exhausting to live in color,
it is so tempting to let it fade.

i have not yet found what i wanted to find
nonetheless;
the silver persists,
because nothing gold can stay.

lemons

when i close my eyes sometimes it feels like the sour world is
spinning on its axis
staying above water is easier in theory than it is in practice
i just hold on with white knuckles until it passes
the aftertaste is always deceivingly delayed
/
my life is just a series of trying to make it through the next
difficult thing
but i suppose so is everybody's
there is no escape from your body
when you can't make it work the right way
/
some days i really hate the cards that i've been dealt
the lemons that life gives are acidic, i'll confess
i've tried but you can't hate yourself back to health
and you can't spend all of your time in the shade
/
to be perfectly concise, i am so mad
i want back the life that i thought i had
making excuses because i don't have the energy to keep plans
none of this has been a fair trade
/
i swallow the pill
in all of its bitter entirety;
i crush up the unproductive guilt
and chase it down with lemonade

the beggar

sometimes i fear
i do not possess the currency that love demands
a claw machine never quite catching its target
an arrow missing its mark
a bird forgotten how to land

a prologue & a eulogy

i. the prologue

can you taste my nervousness?
i'm feeling giddy next to you
our footsteps fall in sync
would bringing up love be too soon?

you showed me childhood photos
and where your family dog is buried
you taught me how to feel truly alive
amidst the feelings i'm trying to learn to carry

i took your touch as a paradigm
the definition of love itself
looking up from beneath the starlight
i told you how i felt

bare feet dancing across floorboards
is it as vivid for you as it is for me?
i wish there was a way to know you're in
the good old days
before they up and leave

does it make you smile to tell our story?
though its pages are weathered and torn
it is still my greatest accomplishment
i wonder if you too would claim it as yours?

a prologue & a eulogy

ii. the eulogy

options

to wake up in the morning
to nourish yourself with food
to open the blinds and try to sing somewhat of a happier
tune

to be the bigger person
to love instead of fear
to hold a space in your heart for those you still wish were
here

to forgive others for their offenses
to make the best choices for yourself
to set boundaries long overdue for your health

to be strong when you feel weak
to put in the effort that you weren't shown
to realize that you were never meant to do all of this alone

i am so tired of having to choose
is this all there is?
choosing to survive over and over and over again?
a trick question with which i make continuous amends

a life full of sorrow is not much of a life at all
what kind of life would it be if we didn't consistently
choose love?

contra

we like the heat of a campfire but fear the spread
of an open flame
we love the sound of the ocean until we're drowning
beneath the waves

we like the chill of the winter air until our fingertips
go numb
we examine the consequences of our own self interest
and then we call it love

we search for a third side to a coin we know has
only two faces
we value routine but often complain about standing
in our places

we yearn for the deepest of passions until deciding we would
rather be alone
we waste up the last of our youth trying not to get old

we are all just hypocrites, imperfectly walking the line
but we can make a difference here, if only we would
try

true love's kiss

once upon a time
in a city as dull & dreamless as this
glittering fantasies are the only antidote
against fitful sleeplessness

so won't you just bear with me
and suspend reality for a while
let's get lost in big ballgowns
and masqueraded smiles

the castle walls would be no match
for the feelings i hold in my heart
we'd dance the entire night away
under a blanket of shining stars

i'd glide down a spiral staircase
and meet your gaze across the ballroom
we'd ride off together on horseback
into the sunset the way that lovers do

i'd hoped we wouldn't end up a tragedy
the likes of romeo & juliet
there's still time before the clock strikes midnight
so come and kiss me like it's life or death

the real world is a cruel wake up call
fairytales don't exist here, not for us
and true love's kiss does not save you
when you're the only one in love

if we're being honest, there's always been a side of you that
favored pain
you seek out petty conflicts like the drama is calling your
name
and later on you'll tell me you had no choice but to enlist;
for some reason my reckless heart always loved you in spite
of this.

you're a soldier that left to fight in an imaginary war,
all of those bitter demons in that traitorous head of yours
and i'm writing all these lonely letters trying to make sense
of why you did it -
for the heartbreak that your departure caused you have not
yet been acquitted.

i paced the floors until i stripped the wood waiting for your
return,
i must face the punishment for being the only one who got
close enough to get burned.
the days pass like molasses; it's been too long since i've
heard your voice
i never dared to tell a soul that i'd made a hopeless kind of
choice.

too young to know any better when i first laid eyes on you
you said we were too naive back then, how could two kids
have possibly decoded some sort of existential truth?

you kept paranoid excuses under the bed stored away like
bullets, ready to be used at any moment
when i turn the lights out it's still just us in the dark: a
disillusioned fighter and his lovesick little poet.

i triple checked the return address before i sent it in the
post
i wondered if you'd been dishonorably discharged, had i
been sending my love to a ghost?
you call yourself a soldier but i fear i am the one who
has more gruesomely fought
i continue writing to you, but i have long since given up
hope for a response.

i still open up the window in the kitchen to let the
sunlight stream in
in hopes that the fresh air will bring your hazel eyes and
honeyed grin back home to me again
and when the curtains blow open with the softest scent of
summer air,
i let myself pretend for a moment that i'd look up and see
you there.

many nights i prayed that you would return victorious
from your make-believe battle
but unfortunately my hope in you has decidedly since
unraveled; this time i cannot forgive.
you left me standing on the platform with a handkerchief
clutched in hand
waiting at the station for a train that may never come
back for me again.

superache

there's an ache between my shoulder blades
where i'm trying to carve out a space to put the blame
it leaves me trembling with the weight of my pain
where the world rests on my shoulders today.

there's an ache that sneaks up through my spine
slithers around the marrow and slips up the sides
i only do what i need to do to survive
i thought these things would get better with time.

there's an ache buried in the soles of my feet
i can't seem to keep them from dragging uselessly
years of providing but never quite getting what i need
i can't keep running on these tired, fickle things.

there's a hairsplitting ache in my head
that makes a home behind my eyelids
i look for hollow cures but nothing seems to soothe it
it's hard to get anything done with all of this heaviness.

but the worst ache of all resides in my chest
the kind that can't be cured by medicine or by rest
i dread the day this heartache finally gets the best
this sorrow has always been an unwelcome guest.

how did i allow it to get this way?
i am too young to be this afraid / drained / in pain
between my chest, my head, my feet, my spine, and my
shoulder blades
there is nowhere left to hide from this relentless
superache.

tran→*slate*

sometimes i worry that you might get your hands on this
and be able to tell it's about you
(*a truth which i would never willingly admit to*)
but you've always had such a simple mind
more drawn to spoonfed visuals than cascading poetry lines
i'll bury my feelings in between references that
soar high above your head
timeless verses personified with careful intent:

i need some of the sensibility that Austen provided, to
become intimately acquainted with both logic and emotion.
Brontë was right when she spoke of punching above your
weight, a petty man fighting to prove yourself too much,
too little, too late.
i am still learning to be bold like Dickinson when it comes
to standing up for myself. i don't have quite as powerful a
voice but i have a voice more confident now nonetheless (*and
it most definitely passes the Bechdel test*).
to be unflinchingly honest the way that Plath always was;
to capture the agony of being alive and all that comes along
with it, all at once.
perhaps i should have been a bit more independent the way
that Alcott described; to march to my own beat is
something i've been dying for ages to try.

the tragedies of shakespeare, homer, and virgil be damned,
you will *not* be the only love i ever have.

so go ahead and go for it, give it the best you can
you still won't be able to decipher it in the end.

love is my native tongue but it's a language you never learned
how to speak;
all i know how to do is write new beginnings and all you
know how to do is leave.

hardly bothered by matters of the heart but always so
predictable; easily entertained,
here's hoping that decoding this verse is easier than it was
trying to get you to stay.

the extra mile

i live my life stuck in the extra mile
exhausted from running a race that isn't mine
an endless parade of trials
tumbling toward the imaginary finish line

the training was relentless
and it never seems to stop
i don't think that i was meant for this
but it wouldn't be the first time i've been wrong

just when i think i'm almost to the end
there's another twist in the road
obstacles intended to break and bend
a secret meaning to decode

i learned the hard way that you get no praise
for using your legs for their intended purpose
even if they're sore and burdened with malaise
if your pain isn't visible, it doesn't exist

everyone runs the race differently
but everyone has to participate
and despite my doubled effort,
i am awarded no sympathy
for finishing too late

untitled

i own the house at the end of the pavement near the cul-de-sac
where i only venture the length of the mailbox and back;
with tall fences and shuttered windows,
a wind chime that resonates in morse code.

each and every shadow shares a similar underscore,
every room severed by lonely, winding corridors;
the wires are all tangled and the outlets spark
i am so tired of the harsh light but terrified of the dark.

i stand isolated amongst all of the wreckage
in a place where faultlessness was once an obsession;
the clock never ceases its ticking, permanently behind,
like the world has somehow frozen but only on the inside.

cracks in the foundation are crawling across the tile
i trace them with tired eyes and the journey feels like miles;
i'm worried that every inspection will produce another grim
diagnosis,
i am the inspector & the repairman & the terrible prognosis.

keep the fridge stocked, keep the bed made, become proficient
in looking the other way
set the table with pristine silverware and meticulously clean
plates;
prepare yourself for guests that never make it through the door
people may come and go but never forget, this mess is *yours.*

the unspoken rules are painted across the walls
etched into the foundation like an imperious memoir:
avoid the filthy fallout and fragments of broken glass
keep your head down and clean up the mess you didn't ask
for.

it would be pointless to bother with looking for a greener
pasture,
sooner or later every selfish facade shatters;
what remains is the inevitable question of whether to evolve
or to mend -
and by the time i've finally chosen, i've got to do it all
again.

this tumultuous storm has been a great deal to endure
i'll admit there are times i do not even want a house
anymore;
i can no longer remember how to make it my own
i do not know how to make it a home.

...

but i will not be the one to turn the lights out
because across the street another set of four walls
stand on their own shaky ground;
evidence of someone else trying to turn a hurricane
into a home
and suddenly i feel a little less alone.

the poet / deconstructed

i wish i was eloquent enough to make you feel what i am feeling in this moment,
to describe in riveting detail the extent of my desperation,
words at the tip of my tongue that escape unbidden, unwilling to adhere to a rhythm;
a truth ready to be divulged that escapes itself somewhere between my mind and the page.

tucked in between freckles and frown lines and the space where my tongue meets the back of my teeth,
a multitude of gathering convictions concealed by a perpetually furrowed brow;
diving into the next one in line with nothing to break the fall,
gathering up reasons to run up a white flag but not quite enough to make a change.

emotions run high like a live-wire headed for short-circuit,
i collect moments in my back pocket to take out and examine later on;
pick them apart until they're nothing but hazy, frenzied fragments
and with the lights burned out, love and fear become interchangeable.

a burst of precipitous vigor with no visible outlet
searching for catharsis like trying to dig a well in the middle of a wasteland;
shoving myself out of my own comfort zone just to see what might come of it all;
i set out on a pursuit of happiness but i suppose i'll settle for something more attainable.

i've studied literature like a language i'd been dying to
memorize,
a slow burn in the dead of winter like a moth to a flame;
the sonnets of my soliloquy echo off the walls of this empty
room,
a summer solstice lit up by fireflies, snuffed out too soon.

i'm already past the precipice, hurtling my way down to
another jagged rock bottom
just so i have an excuse to start over again and pencil in a
different ending this time;
old habits die hard it seems
and so did my billets-doux addressed to you.

i feel like i'm composing the story from back to front,
beginning with the worst parts first,
the words raw and messy like i'm writing them with my left
hand,
with a pen running out of ink, staining me instead
but leaving well enough alone isn't in my repertoire.

i sit in a lonely room stock full of disregarded ideas that
never made it into the light,
each one of them hastily personified;
they fit together and then suddenly they don't anymore,
one moment tethered and the next one torn apart.

walking through cobwebs in the closets, digging through old
memory boxes,
drudging up history from the depths of where i'd buried it;
if i've learned anything at all it's that one truth is glaringly
evident:
i can't afford to be as reckless as i thought I could.

i've fallen down and written myself back up again,
created versions of myself that made an entirely different
array of mistakes;
the ideas run like thick blood through my veins
i trip over my words trying to get them onto a page in a
way that might be understood.

i willingly spill my guts so there's no question about
honesty, i hide my truths in plain sight,
destined to a life of being the one who falls first and
falls harder;
i'm excellent at keeping secrets until i'm faced with a
blank page,
and recounting the mortifying details is like pressing on a
fresh bruise.

i'd tried to craft a fool's paradise but it always ends up a
dystopia instead,
clarity resides just out of reach in my peripherals;
i spend my time romanticizing the past
and praying that i've still got enough pride left to lose.

if you could hear my voice on the page it'd be hoarse
and quiet and frayed,
a sonata set to a rising staccato rhythm,
a heavy melody made for lonely nights and looking out of
rainy windows;
the soundtrack of my life, the only place i have control.

i crumble it up and toss it over my shoulder to begin
once again
another chapter left
untold.

delicate

burrowed in the corner of the attic
in between the silence and the tv static;
an inner monologue softly spoken
echoes of a memoir carefully woven

searching for a place to plant roots
with enough space for the petals to bloom
is seeming to be an impossible feat
always off by a few infinite degrees

i am tired of being strong
and putting effort into things that go so wrong
i want to be able to exhale
without the prerequisites that it seems to entail

when you craft too pristine a mask
it never occurs to anyone to ask
if you're doing okay treading water
or if the days have been getting any harder

just focus on keeping shaking hands still
and making sure the glass looks perpetually halfway filled
just learn to put one foot in front of the next
over and over and over again

applying more pressure does nothing to soothe the ache
for once i want to be something someone might be afraid
to break

would you rather

it's funny how examining the wreckage
really puts things in perspective
the things that were so important to me last october
are either out of reach, wasted dreams, or over

heads i win and tails i lose
but the game's been rigged more than a time or two
if i could rewrite this past year, would the odds have
shifted?
if i threw out the whole chapter, would it have made a
difference?

i've had a few more birthdays to date
but wisdom's got nothing to do with age
and experience doesn't give you any advantage
when you divide up all of the losses and take the average

how many life lessons could've been learned an easier way?
how would the trajectory have changed if i'd have stayed?
it's a high stakes game of would you rather
and i refuse to ask questions to which i don't wish to know
the answer

midas

golden deception drips from your greedy fingers /
scorching even in the dead of winter

your midas touch made you the man of the hour /
drunk on a sense of worthless power

your cup overflows with empty triumphs /
an artifice you've got down to a science

what a lonely life it must be /
to drain those you claim to love so effortlessly

whatever i give you take /
and whatever you touch you break

what you thought was a blessing turned out to be a curse /
a museum of mummified loves, never touched, only observed

graveyard shift

things have been
a little bleak to say the least
it seems happiness is a matter of hit or miss

i've grown apart
from all that i once loved
and isolated myself once again

the darkness beckons
and i'll admit
it's tempting to give in

in all of my life
i've never been this lonely
a spirit set adrift

why is it that
i'm always the one
stuck working the graveyard shift?

jack of all trades

i start out with fragile hope
and all of the best intentions
a variety of pretty half-truths
handcrafted to keep your interest

shuffle all the cards up
and pick one out of the deck
my money's on your entertainment
and it's time to pay my debt

step right up and spin the wheel
it doesn't matter where it ends
i'll do whatever it takes
to capture your undivided attention

you'll have to excuse my arrogance
i'm trying not to be a bore
i learned long ago that if you aren't interesting
your presence becomes a chore

me & my loneliness
still a pitiful party of one;
a jack of every trade
but always a master of none

june, we should've known this was
doomed from the beginning. i had
roots and you had dreams, and you
always said there was never enough
room here to spread your wings.

*letters
to june*

june, did you know they were writing love letters even in the
1700's? it's breathtaking, the way napoleon wrote to
joséphine. they speak so earnestly and i ache to write like
that to you. (wherever you're at, would you write me back?)

june, you've always wanted to get out of this place. who
would i be to take that away? who am i to ask you to stay?

june, we should've stopped it before i fell in too deep. there
is so much i can't give you that you say that you need, but
goodbyes are so hard and you know i'm not good at these
kinds of things.

june, all i could do was soak you up while you were passing
through. i suppose your wish has finally come true, the
summer solstice melted away with hazy memories of you.

june, i promised myself a slow burn and jumped in headfirst,
it's no surprise that i got burned. though i can't say that i
would have done the things you did to me had you been the
one that was in worse. oh well, another lesson learned.

june, i hope you get everything you want out there in the world. the both of us are much better off now i'm sure, but i'd have given anything to stay your girl.

june, it's summer again and i'm right where you left me last year. there's just no escape from you i fear, i can't let this sorry season go by without imagining you here.

june, i know you said you were better off alone. but do you ever feel the way i do when i'm on my own, don't you ever get so lonesome that you can feel it in your bones?

june, so much time stands between us now, tall and wide and uncomfortably loud. you still can't be alone and i still don't do well in big crowds. i can't help wondering what all you've figured out, what all your conversations are about.

june, i'm a different person and i know that you are too. lightyears away from when you first held my hand on the outer loop. i thought about reaching out and checking in but i think it's still too soon.

june, if our time together accomplished anything, i would hope that it made you a little more tender. i would hope that it reminded you that it's okay to remember, even when it hurts, because there's more to this life than either of us could comprehend. maybe in another life we ended up together in the end.

xx

devil's advocate

you used to write scathing sonnets about how much you loathed the finer things in life / champagne glasses & expensive vacations & the social ladders they climb / but as soon as you had the opportunity you cashed in and made the move / to be country-club-cool, your run on sentences punctuated by pretentious words you don't actually know how to use.

you loved to play devil's advocate but there's some buried truth to your words / we hate the things that we wish we had or things we wish we were / because it's something we can afford to do / talk has always been cheap and so is being a fool.

so here goes my cynical sonata that hits all of the wrong notes / i hate the memories and i hate the love and i've hated you the most / when everything's the opposite the lines begin to blur / so let me get it all out before i lose my nerve.

you can't plant roots if you're always searching for greener grass / and you can't breathe in the present if you're still suffocated by the past / your opposition doesn't make anything stronger, it only rips apart / i just hate that the receiving end had to be my heart.

shadow

i am a ghost standing at the foot of my parents bed
asking if i can fall asleep between them once again
what an image i must've been, quiet as a phantom and light as
a feather
learning too quickly that trembling hands are unable to control
the weather

and i've got all of this anger boiling over but pointing fingers
never did me any good
you can't make someone take accountability, even when they
should
the skeletons in my closet quickly became my closest confidants
i learned to stand up on my own two feet, but at what
tiresome cost?

sometimes it doesn't need to be visible bruises and blows
sometimes it's the things that never happened at all that end up
hurting me the most
with the history shoved in my back pocket i try to make
amends
but truthfully it's difficult to see it now through any other lens

so here i sit at the dinner table, this time twenty-two
instead of ten
i've lost count of the changes that have taken place since then
a translucent silhouette of every emotion and moment
myself & the shadow that refuses to remain unnoticed

fight/flight/freeze

bloodshed on a battlefield
a soldier across enemy lines
a million little sacrifices
trying to fight the good fight

an airplane flying over the atlantic
a missed connecting flight
hours of unrelenting turbulence
enclosing a thousand miles

a museum full of statues
moments frozen in time
each one perfectly preserved
choices that were supposed to be mine

(so much of my life feels like it isn't my own
and in the in-betweens i fall behind
i don't want to fight/flight/freeze anymore
i just want to be fine)

but to fight a losing battle is not to lose the war
and sparrows aren't born knowing how to fly
and you can learn a lot from history
if you don't make the same mistakes this time

i put one foot in front of the other
and somehow i make it through the night
i can't always avoid the chaos
but i can always
try

autobiography

if i could see my future
typed out in black and white
i could prepare for the storms a little better
i could map out places to hide

if i knew the joy that was coming
it might make this a little less hard
i would reread my favorite chapters
and skip over all the bad parts

if i had the opus in my hands
i'm afraid it may be too tempting
to skip past the character development
in favor of a hasty happy ending

i would change the conclusion
before i'd even begun;
and when i write the story of my life
my chances are down to one

my memoir will be authentic
well-loved despite its twists & turns
with earmarked pages and writing in all the margins;
a lifetime's worth of my untouched, honest words

faithful

when everything has come crashing down around me
and i can't focus for all of my rushing thoughts
i take comfort in knowing that He has gone before me
and that the pain has come and gone

i will give it all to You
be it a mountain or a mustard seed
be it the good days or the bad
i offer my devotion in its entirety

when i make the hard decisions
i will turn to You as my guide
as the shepherd leads his sheep
so Your heart will forever lead mine

when i am alone with my worries
i will listen for You in the silence
knowing that my prayers are always heard
even when You are quiet

when the world is turned against me
and my heart feels jagged and hateful
i promise You always,
i will be faithful

will your hands craft blessings without
asking for anything in return?
will your words create stories that
encourage and spread hope?
will your arms hold someone else's when
they feel like they're on their own?

will you do your best to find
balance in the chaos?
will your thoughts be productive
and kind?
will your feet forge new paths for those
that follow behind?

will your actions motivate others?
will your testimony inspire hope?
will your eyes reflect the miracles they've
been blessed enough to behold?

will your tears be productive?
will they be reminders that there is
strength in vulnerability?
will the first exhale afterward bring you
the overwhelming warmth of peace?

will your heart continue to love even when
it's difficult?
will you use it to forgive?
will your time be spent wisely, and your
efforts a worthwhile pursuit of it?

will you leave the world a better place than
you found it?
by whose standards will you measure your
success?

though many stand and falsely profess,
only Love can stand the test.

—*SLH*